SOUND
Let's Investigate

by Ruth Owen and Victoria Dobney

Consultant:

Nicky Waller

RUBY TUESDAY BOOKS

Published in 2019 by Ruby Tuesday Books Ltd.

Editor: Mark J. Sachner
Designer: Emma Randall
Production: John Lingham
Proofreader: Evie Croft

Photo credits:
Alamy: 11 (top), 17 (top); FLPA: 14—15, 28—29; Getty Images: 6 (top), 24; NASA: 6 (bottom); Public Domain: 11 (bottom); Ruby Tuesday Books: 15, 17 (bottom); Shutterstock: Cover, 1, 2—3, 4—5, 7, 8—9, 10, 12—13, 16, 18—19, 20 (top), 21, 22, 23 (top), 25 (top), 26—27; SUBPAC: 25 (bottom); Superstock: 20 (bottom), 23 (centre).

ISBN 978-1-78856-041-2

Printed in China by Toppan Leefung Printing Limited

www.rubytuesdaybooks.com

Contents

The download button shows there are free worksheets or other resources available. Go to:
www.rubytuesdaybooks.com/scienceKS2

What's All That Noise?

Drip Drip Drip   *Woof Woof Woof*   *Tweet Tweet*

**A dog barking, people laughing, a phone ringing, the
slam of a door — your world is filled with noise,
or sounds. But what is sound?**

Beeeeep!   *Goodbye!*

Tap Tap Tap

Dinner's Ready!   *Rinnngggggg*

Sound is a type of **energy** that we can hear with our **ears**.

When you strum the strings of a guitar, the strings **vibrate**, or move very fast.
This creates **vibrations** in the **air**. These vibrations are called **sound waves**.

The sound waves travel through the air away from the guitar in every direction.
When your ears pick up the vibrations and send a message to your brain, you
hear the sound of the guitar.

This picture shows how sound
waves act. But you can't actually
see them in the air.

If someone is
playing a guitar next
door, the sound waves
(vibrations) can travel out
of your neighbour's window,
along the street, through
your window (even if it's
closed) and into
your ears.

Waves on the Move

It's tricky to imagine sound waves, but think about what would happen if you dropped a pebble into a pond. Waves in the water would travel away from the pebble. It's the same with sound. The sound waves travel through the air in all directions away from the source of the vibrations.

Let's Talk!

What's your favourite sound? Write down several sentences that describe the sound. Read your description to a partner and see if they can guess the sound.

Buzzzzzzzzzzz

Bumblebee

A bee's buzzing noise is made by its wings vibrating very fast.

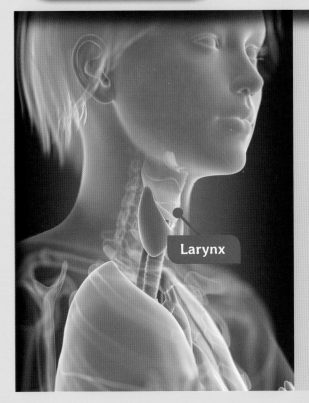

Larynx

Your Voice: What's Vibrating?

Put your fingers gently on your throat and say "Hello". Did you feel vibrations? That's your larynx, or voice box, making the vibrations. The larynx is a short, tube-like structure made of cartilage – the same tough, bendy stuff your ears are made of. Inside the tube are folds of **tissue** called vocal cords. Your vocal cords vibrate as air passes through them. We hear the different strength vibrations as whispering, talking, shouting, singing and laughing.

Investigating Sound

If there was no air on Earth, there would be no sounds around us. That's because sound waves need something to move through.

In the 1600s, an Irish scientist named Robert Boyle devised an experiment to find out if sound waves could travel through a vacuum. A vacuum is a space that contains absolutely nothing — not even air.

Boyle placed a metal bell in a large glass jar. To make the bell ring, he used a magnet on the outside of the jar. Then Boyle pumped all the air out of the jar. Once the jar was a vacuum, the ringing of the bell made no sound.

Boyle proved that sound travels through air, but it cannot travel through a vacuum.

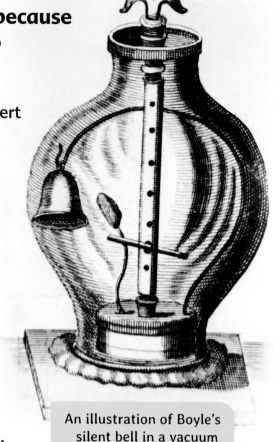

An illustration of Boyle's silent bell in a vacuum

Houston, We Have Silence

If you were an astronaut standing on the Moon, you might hear the voices of your fellow astronauts or instructions from mission control. These sounds would be coming to you through equipment in your air-filled helmet. But if you were to tap two moon rocks together or start the engine of your buggy, there would only be silence. That's because there's no air on the Moon – and no air means no sound waves.

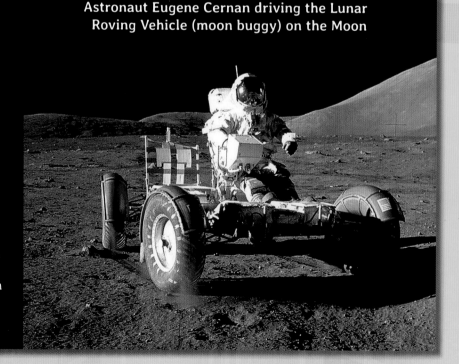

Astronaut Eugene Cernan driving the Lunar Roving Vehicle (moon buggy) on the Moon

What Is an Echo?

Have you ever stood in a large empty room or hallway and shouted, "Hello"? Did you instantly hear a ghostly repeat of the word? That sound is an echo. The sound waves made by your voice **reflected**, or bounced, off the hard walls and came back to you. If you try this in your bedroom, however, there won't be an echo. That's because the carpet, curtains, bed and other objects in the room **absorb** the sound.

Speed of Sound

Sound waves can move fast. In fact, a **sound travels** through the air at **343 metres per second** – that's the length of three football pitches.

Why Does Distance Make Sounds Quieter?

Up close a fire engine's sirens are very loud. But if a fire engine is several streets away, the noise is not as loud. That's because as sound waves travel away from their source (the fire engine) their energy gets spread out. This makes the sounds that reach your ears quieter. The further you are from the source, the quieter the sound will be.

Turn It Up!

A whisper can only be heard if your friend's mouth is close to your ear. A shout, however, can be heard from the other end of a football pitch.

The loudness of a sound depends on the strength or **intensity** of the vibrations.

Strong vibrations make loud sounds, while weak vibrations make quiet or soft sounds.

Volume is a way to describe the loudness of a sound. On a TV remote we increase or decrease the volume to make the sound louder or quieter.

Let's Investigate

How do different-strength vibrations affect sound?

Equipment:
- A small, heavy bowl
- A thick rubber band (one that will fit tightly around the bowl)
- A ruler
- A notebook and pen

Method:

1 Stretch the rubber band around the bowl. Pluck the rubber band.

What kind of sound do you hear?

How could you make the sound louder? What could you do to make it quieter?

2 Write your predictions in your notebook and test them!

3 With one hand, hold the ruler at the edge of a table so about two-thirds of the ruler is hanging over the edge. Flick or twang the ruler.

Describe the sound. How can you make the sound louder or quieter? Record your predictions and test them.

Did your predictions match your results?

What is your conclusion?
Use it to complete this sentence:

A loud sound is made by .... vibrations. A quiet sound is made by .... vibrations.

We can't see sound waves in the air but an electronic instrument called an oscilloscope can help us see them get quieter and louder. The equipment records a sound and then the sound waves are shown on a screen. They look a little like a graph.

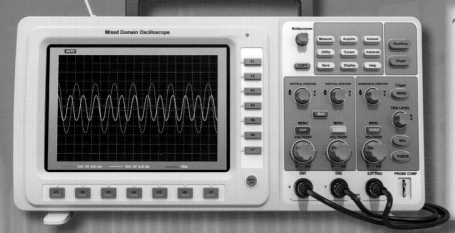

Oscilloscope

This image shows a sound wave on an oscilloscope.

The height of the wave is called its **amplitude**.

This image shows a sound wave that's twice the amplitude (or height) of the one above.

This sound wave would make a much louder sound when it reached our ears.

Let's Test It

Think about these 10 sounds. Then put them in order from quietest to loudest.

- Cat purring
- A pen writing on paper
- A lawnmower
- Your teacher's voice
- An orchestra
- A car horn beeping
- A dog barking
- The hum of a microwave
- A plane taking off
- A bird singing

Now make up your own list of 10 sounds and put them in order.

Loudspeakers

Loudspeakers help to make sounds . . . you guessed it

LOUDER!

The speaker has a part called a cone. The equipment inside the speaker pushes and pulls the cone, making it vibrate back and forth, like the skin of a drum. When the volume is turned up, the cone vibrates a large amount. It makes stronger sound waves that create a louder sound.

Loudspeaker

Cone

How Many Decibels?

The loudness, or volume, of sounds is measured using a unit of measurement called a **decibel**.

A whisper measured in decibels would be about 10 to 20 decibels (dB). At a live music event, a person standing close to the loudspeakers would hear sounds at about 110 dB.

Once noise levels reach 140 dB, they can harm our ears and may even cause **hearing loss**, or **deafness**. Measuring sounds using decibels allows us to know which sounds are safe for our ears and which are dangerous.

How Many Decibels?

Think about the sounds in each of the pictures and then try to match the number of decibels to the pictures.

(The answers are on page 32.)

Normal conversation

Sirens

Food blender

Pneumatic drill

Rustling leaves

Library

100 dB   20 dB   88 dB

40 dB   120 dB   60 dB

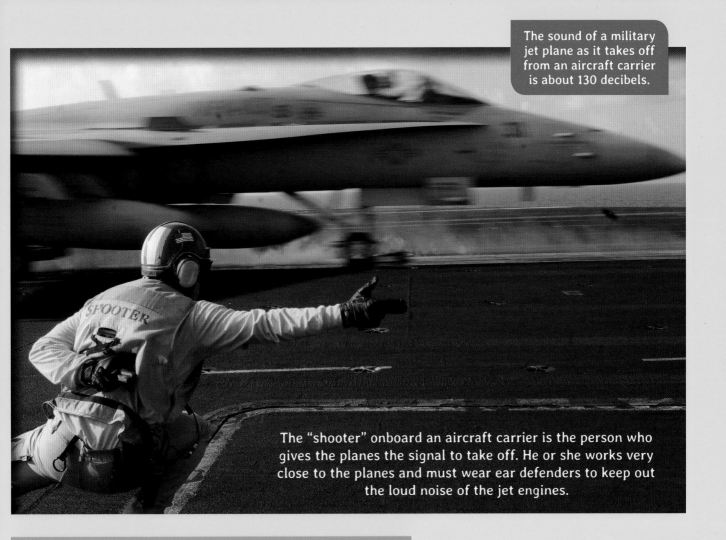

The sound of a military jet plane as it takes off from an aircraft carrier is about 130 decibels.

The "shooter" onboard an aircraft carrier is the person who gives the planes the signal to take off. He or she works very close to the planes and must wear ear defenders to keep out the loud noise of the jet engines.

The First-Ever Telephone

Decibels are named after Alexander Graham Bell, the scientist who invented and made the first-ever working telephone. On 10 March 1876, Bell was testing his latest telephone design. He spoke into the mouthpiece and said:

"Mr. Watson, come here – I want to see you."

These were the first words to ever be spoken on the telephone. Bell's assistant Watson was in another room with the receiver. He proved the telephone worked by repeating the sentence back to Bell.

Bell's sketch of the first-ever working telephone

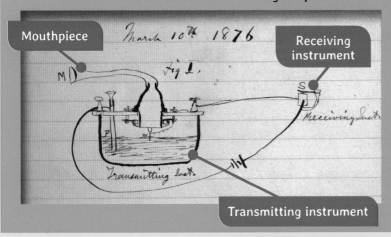

Mouthpiece

Receiving instrument

Transmitting instrument

Protecting Our Ears

People who work with loud equipment, such as pneumatic drills, can suffer damage to their hearing. So can musicians who play loud music and people who work with loud machinery in factories. In these situations people should always wear earplugs or ear defenders to block out noise and protect their hearing.

11

High or Low?

Some noises, like a squeaky dog toy or a baby's cry, are high-pitched. Others, like the rumble of thunder or notes played on a tuba, are low-pitched.

The **pitch** of a sound is all to do with how many vibrations the source of the sound makes per second. The number of vibrations per second is the sound's **frequency**.

Long and Short

The long bars on a xylophone make low-pitched sounds when they are hit with a mallet. That's because long objects make slow vibrations. The short bars vibrate more quickly, which makes a higher-pitched sound.

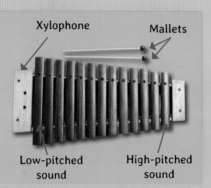

Xylophone

Mallets

Low-pitched sound

High-pitched sound

Let's Investigate

What makes a sound high-pitched or low-pitched?

Equipment:
- A long rubber band
- A ruler
- A pencil
- A notebook and pen

Method:

1 Stretch the rubber band lengthwise over the ruler.

2 Slide a pencil under the rubber band about 5 cm from one end of the ruler.

3 Hold the ruler and pluck the middle of the long section of the rubber band.

What kind of sound do you hear?

4 Now pluck the short section of rubber band.

Does this noise sound higher or lower than the first?

Where would you pluck the rubber band to make a very low sound?

Where would you position the pencil and then pluck to make a very high sound?

5 Write your predictions in your notebook, test them and record your results.

What do you notice about the rubber band when it makes a high-pitched sound? How about when it makes a low-pitched sound?

(There are some answers on page 32.)

Investigating Frequency

We can use an oscilloscope to see the frequency (number of vibrations per second) of a sound wave.

This sound wave has high peaks and troughs that are spread out. It would make a loud, low-pitched sound.

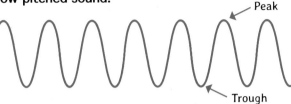

Peak

Trough

This sound wave has double the frequency (number of peaks and troughs). It sounds as loud as the first wave but its pitch is higher because it has twice as many vibrations per second.

A person's voice can be high-pitched or low-pitched.

Making Music with Water

Equipment:
• 5 or more identical glasses
• A jug of water
• A teaspoon
• A notebook and pen

Method:

1 Line up the five glasses. Pour about 2.5 cm of water into the first glass. Fill the last glass nearly to the top.

2 Now pour different amounts of water into the other three glasses.

3 Use the spoon to gently tap the glass that contains the least amount of water on its side.

Did the glass make a high-pitched or low-pitched sound?

What kind of sound do you think the full glass of water will make? What about the other glasses?

4 Write your predictions in your notebook and test them.

Did your results match your predictions?

5 Arrange the glasses so they are in order from the lowest-pitched to the highest-pitched. Try making up a tune to play on your water instrument!

(There are some answers on page 32.)

Sounds on the Move

To reach our ears, vibrations, or sound waves, must travel from the source of the vibrations through something. When you shout across a football pitch, the sound waves travel through air.

But can sound waves travel through solids?

Let's Test It

Ask a partner to scribble on some paper at the other end of a table from where you are sitting. Listen to the sound it makes. Now put your ear to the table and get them to scribble again. Is the sound louder or quieter?

Humpback whale mother and calf

Sounds travel better through solids than through air, so they sound louder. Sounds also travel better through water than through air.

Long-Distance Singing

Humpback whales communicate in the ocean by grunting, moaning, shrieking and making blasts of noise. Their sounds, or songs, travel for long distances. Scientists estimate that some of the whales' sound waves may travel underwater for 2500 kilometres – and possibly even further!

Air, liquids such as water and solids are made up of tiny **molecules**. If you could see the molecules they would look a little like this.

Air molecules are mostly made up of gases. There are spaces between the molecules.

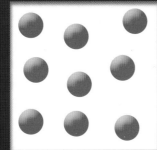

Water molecules are closer together than air molecules.

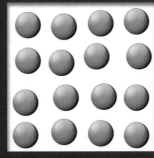

The molecules in a solid are packed tightly together.

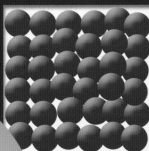

The molecules in water are closer together than in air. This allows sound waves to move through them much faster than through air molecules. The molecules in a solid are even closer together. Sound waves can move through a solid faster than through air or water.

Speed of Sound

How fast do sounds travel through different substances?

Air:	343 metres per second
Water:	1493 metres per second
Wood:	3000 to 5000 metres per second
Steel:	5130 metres per second

Let's Investigate

How well do sound waves travel through solids?

Equipment:
- A piece of string about 70 cm long
- A wire coat hanger
- A table
- A partner
- A notebook and pen

Method:

1. Tie the centre of the string around the hook of the coat hanger.

2. Ask your partner to loosely tie each end of the string to your index fingers.

3. Gently tap the coat hanger against the edge of the table.

How would you describe the sound? Is it loud or quiet?

4. Now gently put your index fingers in your ears and tap the coat hanger on the table again.

How does this sound compare to the first?

5. Record your results in your notebook.

Was the sound louder when it travelled through air or through the solid string?

Write a description of how the sound waves reached your ears both times you tapped the coat hanger on the table.

How Do We Hear?

Your ears are the hardworking organs that capture sound waves and give you your sense of hearing.

The outside wrinkly part of your ear on the side of your head is called the **auricle**. It is made of tough, rubbery tissue called cartilage. The auricle collects sound waves and guides them into a tube called the **ear canal**.

The sound waves travel down your ear canal until they hit your **eardrum**. The eardrum is a piece of skin that is tightly stretched across the ear canal — a little like the skin on a drum.

The sound waves make your eardrum vibrate.

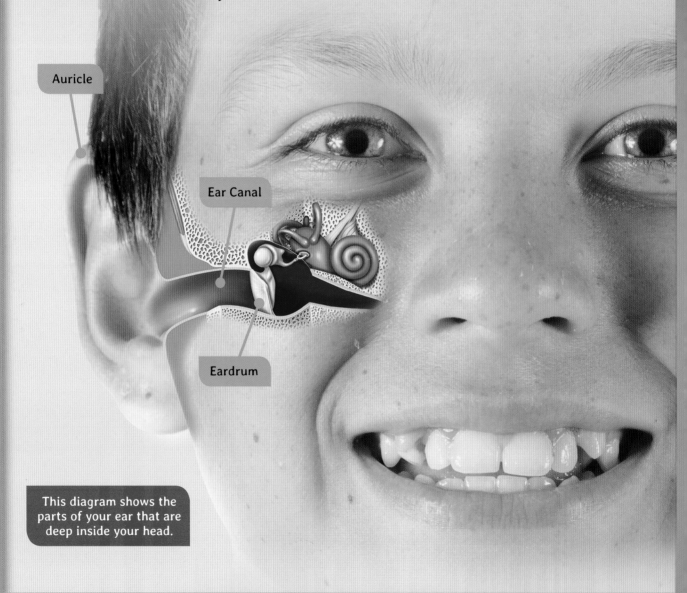

Auricle

Ear Canal

Eardrum

This diagram shows the parts of your ear that are deep inside your head.

Having an ear on each side of your head allows you to collect sound waves coming at you from both sides.

Let's Investigate

How do eardrums work?

In this investigation you're going to make a model of your eardrum using items you can find in a kitchen!

Equipment:
- A ceramic bowl
- Cling film
- A saucepan lid
- A metal spoon
- Some sugar
- A notebook and pen

Method:

1. Tightly stretch some cling film over the top of the bowl.

2. Hold the saucepan lid about 15 cm from the bowl. Watch the model eardrum and bang the lid with a metal spoon.

Did you observe anything happening to the eardrum?

3. Sprinkle about half a teaspoon of sugar onto the model eardrum.

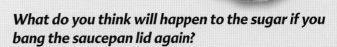

What do you think will happen to the sugar if you bang the saucepan lid again?

4. Write your prediction in your notebook. Then bang the lid while observing your model.

What do you observe? Write down your results. Did your predictions match what happened?

How does what you observed support the idea that sound waves make an eardrum vibrate?

Inside Your Ear

Sound waves enter your ear and make your eardrum vibrate. What happens next?

Your eardrum passes on the vibrations to a tiny bone called the malleus. Next, the malleus moves and hits a bone called the incus. Finally, the incus passes on the vibrations to the stapes bone.

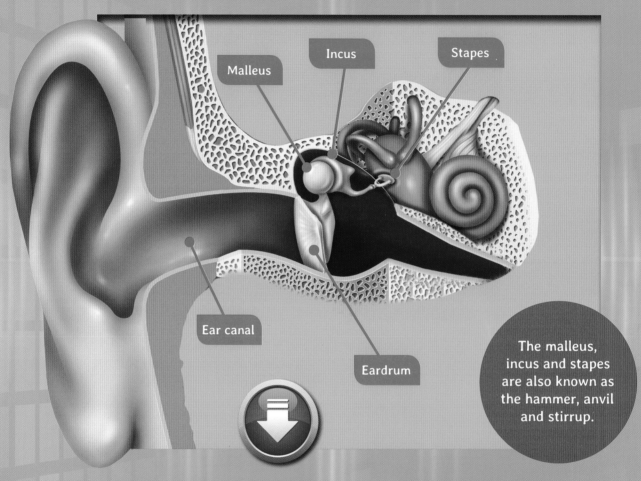

Malleus

Incus

Stapes

Ear canal

Eardrum

The malleus, incus and stapes are also known as the hammer, anvil and stirrup.

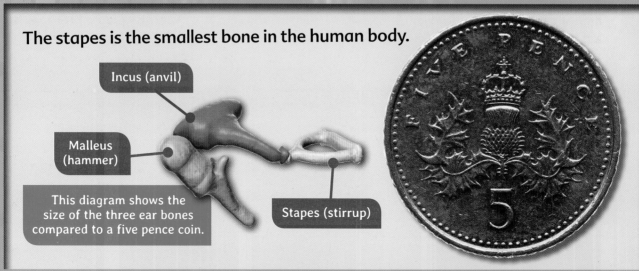

The stapes is the smallest bone in the human body.

Incus (anvil)

Malleus (hammer)

Stapes (stirrup)

This diagram shows the size of the three ear bones compared to a five pence coin.

Sound waves are travelling all around us. We often don't even notice the many sounds that are entering our ears.

Close your eyes now. What sounds can you hear? Are they loud or quiet? Low-pitched or high-pitched?

What might these everyday noises look like when recorded on an oscilloscope?

(Look back to pages 9 and 13. How are loud and quiet sound waves shaped? How are high-pitched and low-pitched sound waves shaped?)

DING DONG!

A doorbell is often made up of two tones – DING DONG! Both are the same volume, but each one has a different pitch. If a doorbell is recorded on an oscilloscope, the sound wave might look something like this.

The two different sounds the doorbell makes are the same volume because the heights of the waves are all the same. However, there are two different pitches.

The first sound is higher-pitched so the waves are more frequent and closer together.

The second sound is lower-pitched so the waves are less frequent and further apart.

Look at these images. Consider the noises in the pictures and how they might look if they were recorded on an oscilloscope. In a notebook, draw what you think each sound would look like.
Can a friend match up which sound wave represents each sound?

From Your Ears to Your Brain

Once vibrations pass through the three tiny bones in your ear, what happens next?

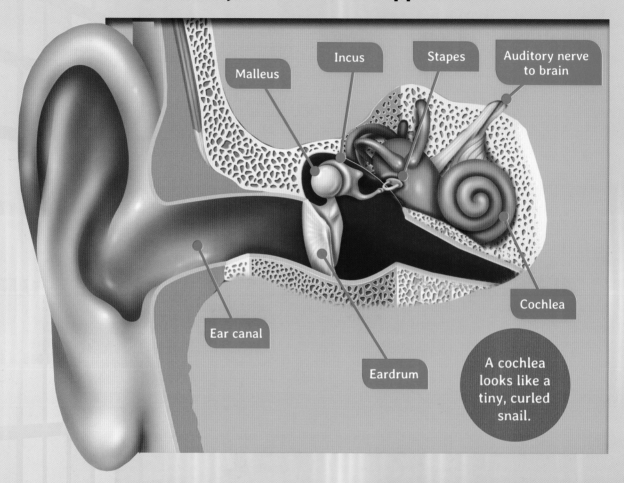

Malleus

Incus

Stapes

Auditory nerve to brain

Ear canal

Eardrum

Cochlea

A cochlea looks like a tiny, curled snail.

The stapes bone vibrates against a part of your ear called the **cochlea**. The cochlea is filled with liquid and contains about 15,000 **microscopic** hairs.

Inside the cochlea the vibrations from the stapes make ripples in the liquid. The tiny hairs are moved by the ripples and turn the movement into messages.

Finally, the messages travel along the **auditory nerve** to your brain. In an instant your brain turns the messages into a sound that you hear.

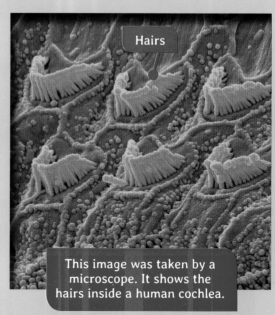

Hairs

This image was taken by a microscope. It shows the hairs inside a human cochlea.

Let's Investigate

Double bass

Take a look at these musical instruments.

What might affect the pitch and volume of each instrument?

Mbira

Hammered dulcimer

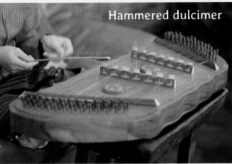

Steel pans

Can you make an instrument?

Make an instrument that can play a variety of pitches and volumes. Before you begin, do some revision by looking back to the investigations on pages 12 and 13.

Equipment:
- Rubber bands of various size and thickness
- Junk modelling materials, including: cardboard boxes, plastic containers and paper towel tubes

Method:

1 Look carefully at your materials and think about your design.

How could the materials be used to create an instrument with controllable volume and pitch? How will you play your instrument — for example, pluck it or hit it with a beater?

2 Write down your ideas and a method for making your instrument.

3 Now try making your instrument following your method. Experiment with and adapt your instrument, recording which parts of your design are successful.

How did you change the pitch and volume of your instrument? Are there other ways to do this?

Help with Hearing

Not everyone hears the sounds around them in the same way. Some people have hearing loss.

Hearing loss, or deafness, can happen if an injury or illness affects a person's ears. Some people are born with hearing loss.

A person with hearing loss might be able to hear some sounds but not others. Some people are **profoundly deaf**, which means they cannot hear any sounds at all.

Sign Language

Many people with hearing loss and their friends and families communicate with sign language. They talk using hand shapes, movements of their bodies and facial expressions.

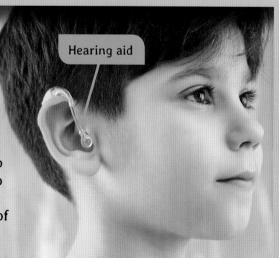

Hearing aid

Hearing Aids

Sometimes a deaf person's ears need help in passing vibrations to the cochlea. A hearing aid on the outside part of the ear can do this.

An infection called meningitis can sometimes lead to hearing loss. This is because the infection spreads to the cochlea and damages the tiny hairs inside. Once the hairs are damaged, it makes it more difficult for vibrations to be received and passed on through the cochlea.

Cochlear Implants

Some people with damaged cochleas have an operation. A doctor puts a tiny piece of equipment called a cochlear implant inside their cochlea. The implant does the job of the tiny hairs and sends messages to the brain along the auditory nerve. Equipment on the outside of the head helps, too.

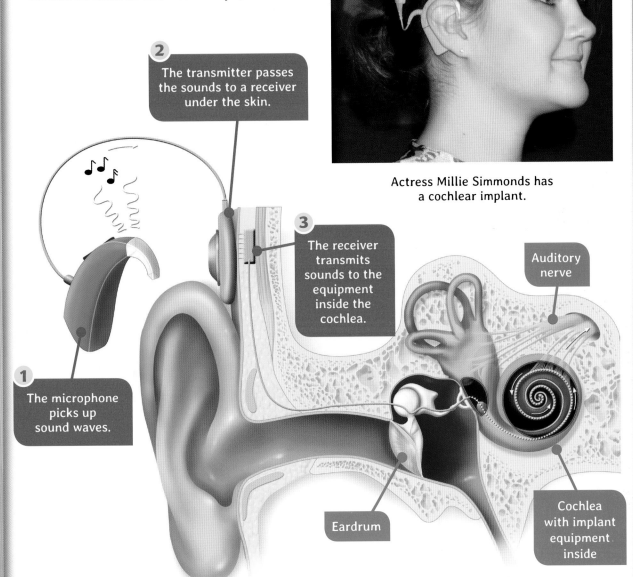

Actress Millie Simmonds has a cochlear implant.

2 The transmitter passes the sounds to a receiver under the skin.

3 The receiver transmits sounds to the equipment inside the cochlea.

Auditory nerve

1 The microphone picks up sound waves.

Eardrum

Cochlea with implant equipment inside

Take Care of Your Ears

- Earwax usually washes out of your ears when you wash your hair. Don't try to remove it with a cotton bud or finger.

- Very loud sounds can damage your ears. When you wear earphones, keep the volume turned down low.

- If your ears hurt or you are having trouble hearing, tell one of the people who take care of you right away.

- And finally . . . .
  NEVER POKE ANYTHING IN YOUR EARS!

Incredible Ability

Evelyn Glennie is the world's first professional solo percussionist. She composes music and performs around the world. She is also profoundly deaf.

Evelyn had lost most of her hearing by the age of 12. But with her percussion teacher she challenged what it means to hear and play music.

Evelyn understood that hearing music wasn't just limited to how her ears functioned. She would place her hands on the wall to feel vibrations coming from music being played in the room. By doing this, she learned how to detect the smallest differences between one note and the next.

Percussionists play instruments such as drums, maracas and xylophones.

Evelyn playing at the opening ceremony of the 2012 Olympic Games in London

Evelyn's sense of touch is her own special form of listening. Rather than depending on sound vibrations passing through her ears, she feels musical vibrations using her entire body. She often performs barefoot so she can feel vibrations through the stage.

Evelyn's incredible skills have helped change the mindset of the music industry to focus on musical ability rather than someone's disability.

Let's Test It

Take a drum and rest one of your hands on it. Use the other hand to bang and tap the drum in a variety of places and with different amounts of force. Does it seem that you can "hear" the sound the drum makes with your resting hand? And does the drum sound different through your hand when you change how you bang it?

Chris Fonseca

Chris Fonseca is a professional Lyrical Hip Hop dancer and dance teacher. As a toddler he contracted meningitis, which left him profoundly deaf. Chris has a cochlear implant, but he has also developed his own ways to "hear" music. Chris touches the loud speakers with his hands and feels the vibrations travel up his arms and through his body. He also studies the lyrics of songs. This helps him become part of the music and make sense of its rhythm and beat.

Chris sometimes uses a SUBPAC. This is a special backpack that enables the wearer to feel the vibrations coming from music through their skin, muscles and bones.

SUBPAC backpack

Hearing with Ultrasound

Our ears can detect millions of sounds. But some sounds are too high-pitched for humans to hear. This kind of sound is called ultrasound.

The number of vibrations per second made by a sound wave is its frequency. We measure frequency using units of measurement called **hertz** (Hz).

If a sound has a frequency that's higher than 20,000 hertz, it is ultrasound. Many animals, including cats, dogs and bats, can hear ultrasound. However, ultrasound is too high-pitched for humans to hear.

The human ear can hear as low as 20 hertz and as high as 20,000 hertz.

Seeing with Sound

Ultrasound is used to check on the health of unborn babies. Ultrasound waves, or vibrations, are transmitted into the mother's body using an ultrasound probe. The waves reflect off the baby and back into a computer, where they form a picture.

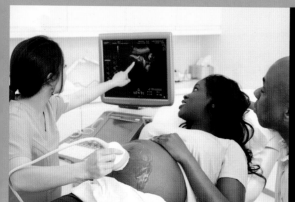

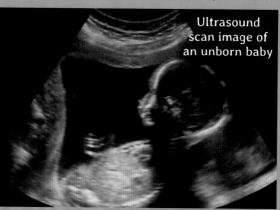

Ultrasound scan image of an unborn baby

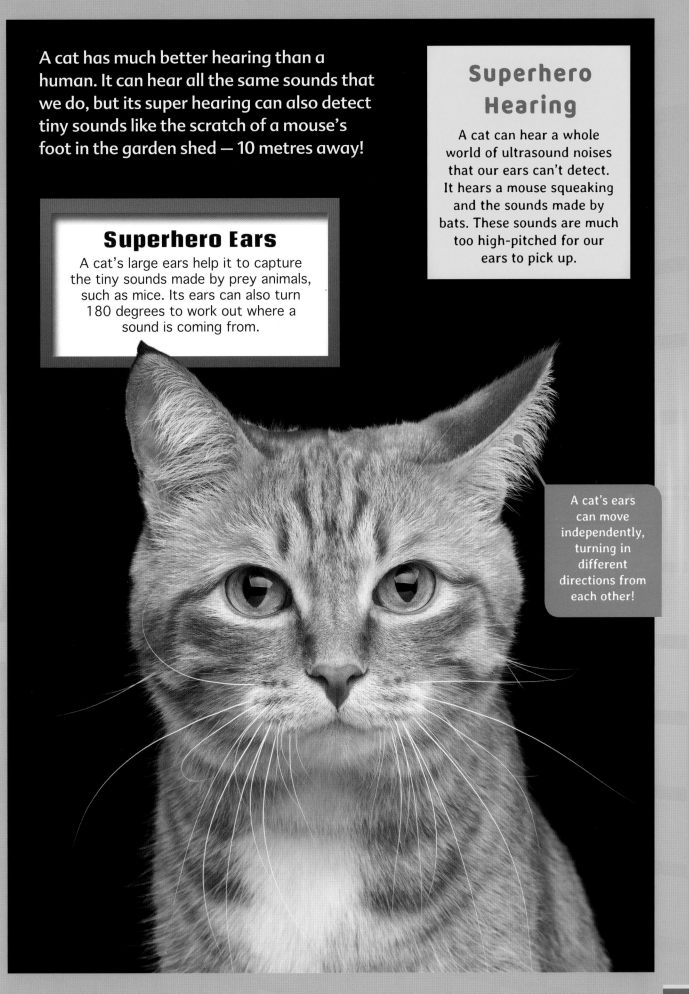

A cat has much better hearing than a human. It can hear all the same sounds that we do, but its super hearing can also detect tiny sounds like the scratch of a mouse's foot in the garden shed — 10 metres away!

Superhero Hearing

A cat can hear a whole world of ultrasound noises that our ears can't detect. It hears a mouse squeaking and the sounds made by bats. These sounds are much too high-pitched for our ears to pick up.

Superhero Ears

A cat's large ears help it to capture the tiny sounds made by prey animals, such as mice. Its ears can also turn 180 degrees to work out where a sound is coming from.

A cat's ears can move independently, turning in different directions from each other!

Hunting with Sound

Humans use sound to hear the world. But some animals actually use sound to build up a picture of their world — and to help them hunt.

Some types of bats hunt for moths and other flying insects using a system called **echolocation**. As a bat flies through the darkness, it makes ultrasonic sounds. These sound waves bounce off an insect (like an echo) and return to the bat.

The sound waves tell the bat where its prey is located and how far away. Then the bat chases its prey.

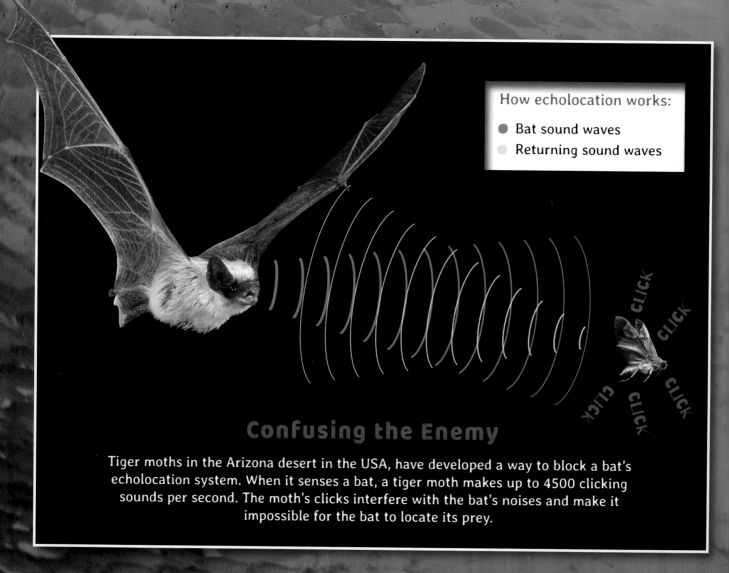

How echolocation works:
- Bat sound waves
- Returning sound waves

CLICK CLICK CLICK CLICK CLICK CLICK

Confusing the Enemy

Tiger moths in the Arizona desert in the USA, have developed a way to block a bat's echolocation system. When it senses a bat, a tiger moth makes up to 4500 clicking sounds per second. The moth's clicks interfere with the bat's noises and make it impossible for the bat to locate its prey.

It's difficult to see very far underwater, so dolphins use echolocation to hunt for fish. A dolphin sends out clicking sounds into the water. When the sounds hit something, such as a fish, they bounce back to the dolphin as echoes.

The echoes tell the dolphin how far away the fish is, its size, its shape and even its speed.

Clicking for Dinner

Dolphins send out clicks from the rounded fatty part of their foreheads. This is called the melon. They pick up the returning echoes as vibrations through their lower jaws.

Glossary

absorb
To take in or soak up.

air
The invisible mixture of gases that is all around us. Air contains the gas oxygen that people and animals need to breathe.

amplitude
The strength of a sound wave; also, the height of a sound wave when seen on a graph.

auditory nerve
A bundle of nerve cells that carry information from the cochlea to the brain.

auricle
The part of your ear that sticks out from the side of your head. It is made from cartilage.

cochlea
The part of your inner ear that contains liquid and hairs that send messages to your brain and help create sounds.

deafness
See "hearing loss".

decibel
A unit of measurement used to measure the loudness of a sound.

ear
An organ in the body of a person or animal that is used for hearing.

ear canal
A narrow tube that connects the outside part of your ear to the inner parts of your ear.

eardrum
A piece of skin that is stretched tightly across your ear canal, like the tightly stretched top of a drum.

echolocation
A system in which an animal makes a sound that reflects off an object and then returns to the animal. Echolocation is used by some animals to find prey.

energy
The force that allows things to move and happen. There are different types of energy, such as sound energy, light energy and electrical energy.

frequency
The number of vibrations per second made by a source of sound.

hearing loss
Being unable to hear some sounds or all sounds. Hearing loss, or deafness, happens if one or more parts of a person's ears are not working as they should.

hertz
The unit of measurement that measures the frequency of sound wave vibrations.

intensity
The strength of something — for example, vibrations.

microscopic
Too small to see with the eyes alone; only visible through a microscope.

molecule
A group of atoms that are bonded together. For example, a water molecule (H_2O) is made of two hydrogen atoms and one oxygen atom. Everything is made of atoms and they are the smallest particles of any object or substance.

organ
A part of the body that has a particular job to do.

pitch
How high or low a sound is — for example, a whistle is high-pitched and a dumper truck's engine is low-pitched.

profoundly deaf
Unable to hear any sounds at all.

reflect
To throw back and not absorb. For example, a mirror reflects light and bare walls reflect sound.

sound waves
Vibrations that are collected by your ears and turned into sounds.

tissue
A group of connected cells in your body that work together. Cells are very tiny parts of a living thing.

ultrasound
Sound waves that are too high-pitched to be detected by human hearing.

vibrate
To move quickly back and forth or side to side.

vibrations
Quick back-and-forth shaking movements that can be felt or heard.

volume
The loudness of a sound.

Index

Answers

Page 10:
Rustling leaves 20 dB; Library 40 dB; Normal conversation 60 dB; Food blender 88 dB; Pneumatic drill 100 dB; Sirens 120 dB.

Page 12:
The short, tightly stretched section of rubber band made fast vibrations and a high-pitched sound. The long, looser section of rubber band vibrated more slowly and made a low-pitched sound.

Page 13:
The glass that contained the least water made a high-pitched sound. That's because it acted like a short object and vibrated fast, creating a high-pitched sound. The full glass acted like a long object, vibrating slowly and making a low-pitched sound.